KRISHNAMURTI

The Song of Life

HORACE LIVERIGHT · INC.

New York

COPYRIGHT 1931
THE STAR PUBLISHING TRUST
EERDE OMMEN, HOLLAND
Translation Rights Reserved

FOREWORD

The attainment of Truth is an absolute, final experience. I have re-created myself after Truth. I am not a poet; I have merely attempted to put into words the manner of my realization.

KRISHNAMURTI

THE SONG OF LIFE

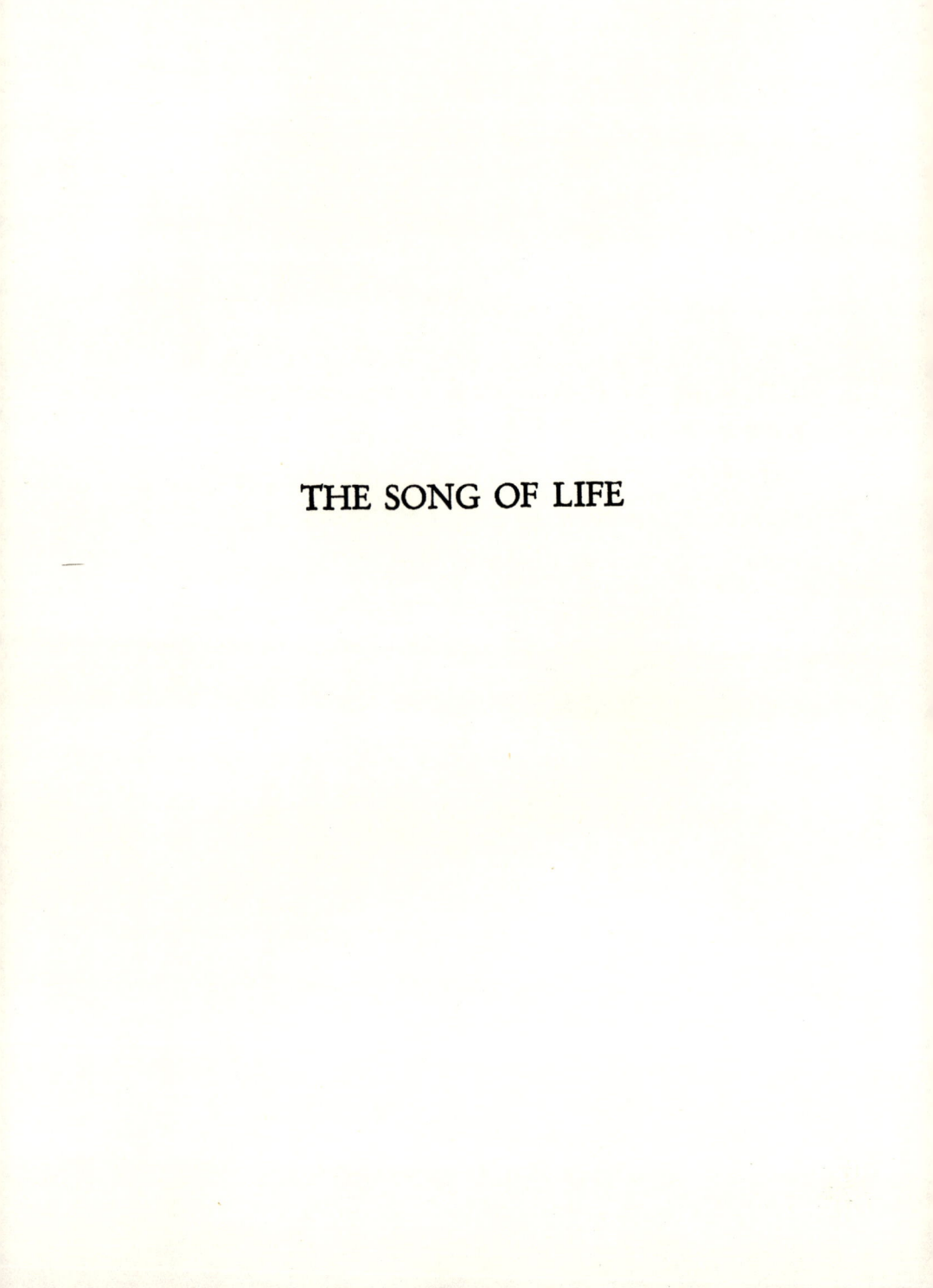

I

Make of thy desire the desire of the world,
Of thy love the love of the world.
In thy thoughts take the world to thy mind,
In thy doings let the world behold thine eternity.

Thou mayest draw the many waters of a well,
But thou canst not quench the thirst of thy desires.
Thy heart may hold the flower of its love,
But with the coming of death the flower fadeth.
Thy thoughts may soar to lofty purpose,
But with anxious conflict they are caught in bondage.

As an arrow shot by a strong arm,
So let thy purpose strike deep into the everlasting.
As the mountain stream, pure in its swiftness,
So let thy mind race eagerly towards freedom.

Awakened from the heart of love,
My voice is the voice of understanding,
Born of infinite sorrow.

II

Who can say if thy heart be clean?
Who can tell thee if thy mind be pure?
Who can give thee the satisfaction of thy desire?
Who can heal thee of the burning pain of satisfaction?
Shall understanding be given
Or the way of love be shown to thee?
Shalt thou escape that fear which men call death?
Canst thou put away the ache of loneliness
Or run from the cry of anxiety?
Canst thou hide thyself behind the laughter of music
Or lose thyself in merry rejoicings?

Wisdom shall be born of understanding.
She putteth forth her voice
In the wilderness of utter confusion.

A man saw the dancing shadows
And went in search of the cause of so much beauty.

Can Life die?
Look into the eye of thy neighbour.

The valley lies hidden in the darkness of a
    cloud
But the mountain top is serene
In its gaze of the open sky.

On the banks of a holy river
A pilgrim repeats a ceaseless chant,
And cloistered in a cool temple
A man kneels, lost in a devout whisper.
But, behold, under the heavy dust of summer
Lies a green leaf.

Who shall call thee out of thy prison house?
Or tear away the bondage from thine eye?
A path mounts slowly up the mountain side
But who shall carry thee as his burden?

I saw a lame man coming towards me,
I shed tears of aching memory.

In the far distance
A lone star holds the sky.

III

The end is in the beginning of all things,
Suppressed and hidden,
Awaiting to be released through the rhythm
Of pain and pleasure.

Caught in the agony of Time,
Maimed by the inward stress of growth,
O Beloved,
The Self of which thou art the whole
Is seeking the way of illumined ecstasy.

Fashioned in the poetry of balance,
Gathering the riches of life's pursuit,
O Beloved,
The Self of which thou art the whole
Is making its way to the heart of all things.

In the secret sanctuary of desire,
Through the recesses of enfolding love,
O Beloved,
The Self of which thou art the whole
Dances to the Song of Eternity.

By the visible and invisible infinity,
In the round of birth and death,
O Beloved,
The Self of which thou art the whole
Is bridging the space of separation.

Confused in fervent worship,
Deluded by the vain pursuits of thought,
O Beloved,
The Self of which thou art the whole
Is being fused into the Incorruptible.

As ever, O Beloved,
The Self is still the whole.

IV

Listen, O friend,
I will tell thee of the secret perfume of Life.

Life has no philosophy,
No cunning systems of thought.

Life has no religion,
No adoration in deep sanctuaries.

Life has no god,
Nor the burden of fearsome mystery.

Life has no abode,
Nor the aching sorrow of ultimate decay.

Life has no pleasure, no pain,
Nor the corruption of pursuing love.

Life is neither good nor evil,
Nor the dark punishment of careless sin.

Life gives no comfort,
Nor does it rest in the shrine of oblivion.

Life is neither spirit nor matter,
Nor is there the cruel division of action and
　　inaction.

Life has no death,
Nor has it the void of loneliness in the shadow
　　of Time.

Free is the man who lives in the Eternal,
For Life is.

V

A thousand eyes with a thousand views,
A thousand hearts with a thousand loves,
Am I.

As the sea that receiveth
The clean and the impure rivers
And heedeth not,
So am I.

Deep is the mountain lake,
Clear are the waters of the spring,
And my love is the hidden source of things.

Ah, come hither and taste of my love.
Then, as of a cool evening
The lotus is born,
Shalt thou find thy heart's own secret desire.

The scent of the jasmin fills the night air;
Out of the deep forest
Comes the call of a passing day.

The Life of my love is unburdened;
The attainment thereof is the freedom of
    fulfilment.

VI

Love is its own divinity.
If thou shalt follow it,
Putting aside the weary burden
Of a cunning mind,
Thou shalt be free of the fear
Of anxious love.

Love is not hedged about
By space and time,
By joyless things of the mind.
Such love delights in the heart
Of him who has richly wandered
In the confusion of love's own pursuits.

The Self, the Beloved,
The hidden loveliness of all things,
Is love's immortality.

Oh, why needst thou seek further,
Why further, friend?
In the dust of careless love
Lies Life's endless journey.

VII

Love Life.
Neither the beginning nor the end
Knows whence it comes.
For it has no beginning and no end.
Life is.

In the fulfilling of Life there is no death,
Nor the ache of great loneliness.
The voice of melody, the voice of desolation,
Laughter and the cry of sorrow
Are but Life on its way to fulfilment.

Look into the eyes of thy neighbour
And find thyself with Life,
Therein is immortality,
Life eternal, never changing.

For him who is not in love with Life,
There is the anxious burden of doubt
And the lone fear of solitude;
For him there is but death.

Love Life,
And thy love shall know of no corruption.
Love Life, and thy judgment shall uphold thee.
Love Life; thou shalt not wander away
From the path of understanding.

As the fields of the earth are divided,
Man makes a division of Life,
And thereby creates sorrow.

Worship not the ancient gods
With incense and flowers;
But Life with great rejoicing;
Shout in the ecstasy of joy
There is no entanglement in the dance of Life.

I am of that Life, immortal, free,
The Eternal Source.
Of that Life I sing.

VIII

Seek not the perfume of a single heart
Nor dwell in its easeful comfort;
For therein abides
The fear of loneliness.

I wept,
For I saw
The loneliness of a single love.

In the dancing shadows
Lay a withered flower.

The worship of many in the one
Leads to sorrow.
But the love of the one in many
Is everlasting bliss.

IX

How easily
The tranquil pool is disturbed
By the passing winds.

Nay, friend,
Seek not thy happiness
In the fleeting.

There is but one way;
That path lies in thyself,
Through thine own heart.

X

A dream comes through a multitude of desires.
When the mind is tranquil
Undisturbed by thought,
When the heart is chaste
With the fullness of love uncorrupted,
Then shalt thou discover,
O friend,
A world beyond the illusion of words.

Therein is unity of all Life.
Therein is the silent Source,
Which sustains the dancing worlds.

In that world there is neither heaven nor hell,
Past, present nor future;
Neither the deception of thought,
Nor the soft whisperings of dying love.

Oh, seek that world
Where death does not dance in its shadowless
    ecstasy,

Where the manifestations of Life
Are as the shadows that the smooth lake holds.

It lies about thee
And without thee it exists not.

XI

As out of the deep womb of a mountain
Is born a swift-running stream;
So out of the aching depths of my heart
Has come forth joyous love,
The perfume of the world.

Through the sunlit valleys rush the waters,
Entering lake upon lake,
Ever wandering, never still;
So is my love,
Emptying itself from heart to heart.

As the waters move sadly
Through the dark, cavernous valley;
So has my love become dull
Through the shame of easy desire.

As the tall trees are destroyed
By the strong rush of waters
That have nourished their deep roots;
So has my love torn cruelly
The heart of its rejoicing.

I have shattered the very rock on which I grew.
And as the wide river
Now escapes to the dancing sea,
Whose waters know no bondage;
So is my love in the perfection of its freedom.

XII

Oh, rejoice!
There is thunder among the mountains,
And long shadows lie across the green face of the valley.

The rains
Bring forth green shoots
Out of the dead stumps of yesterday.
High among the rocks
An eagle is building his nest.

All things are great with Life.

O friend,
Life fills the world.
Thou and I are in eternal union.

Life is as the waters
That satisfy the thirst of kings and beggars alike:
The golden vessel for the king,
For the beggar the potter's vessel,
Which breaks to pieces at the fountain.
Each holds his vessel dear.

There is loneliness,
There is fear of solitude,
The ache of a dying day,
The sorrow of a passing cloud.

Life, destitute of love,
Wanders from house to house,
With none to declare its loveliness.

Out of the granite rock
Is fashioned a graven image
Which men hold sacred;
But they tread carelessly the rock
On the way
That leads to the temple.

O friend,
Life fills the world.
Thou and I are in eternal union.

XIII

Search out the secret pursuit of thy desire;
Then thou shalt not live in illusion.

What canst thou know of happiness,
If in the vale of misery thou hast not walked?
What canst thou know of freedom,
If against thy bondage thou hast not cried aloud?
What canst thou know of love,
If from the entanglement of love
Thou has not sought deliverance?

I saw the flowers blossom
In the dark hours of a still night.

XIV

Does the raindrop hold in its fullness
The raging stream?
Does the raindrop in its loneliness
Feed the solitary tree on the hill?
Does the raindrop in its great descent
Create the sweet sound of many waters?
Does the raindrop in its pureness
Quench the aching thirst?

It is the unwise who chase
The shadow of self in Life.
And Life eludes them,
For they wander in the ways of bondage.

Wherefore the struggle in loneliness of division?
In Life there is neither you nor I.

XV

I have no name;
I am as the fresh breeze of the mountains.
I have no shelter;
I am as the wandering waters.
I have no sanctuary, like the dark gods;
Nor am I in the shadow of deep temples.
I have no sacred books;
Nor am I well-seasoned in tradition.

I am not in the incense
Mounting on high altars,
Nor in the pomp of ceremonies.
I am neither in the graven image
Nor in the rich chant of a melodious voice.

I am not bound by theories
Nor corrupted by beliefs.
I am not held in the bondage of religions,
Nor in the pious agony of their priests.
I am not entrapped by philosophies,
Nor held in the power of their sects.

I am neither low nor high,
I am the worshipper and the worshipped.
I am free.

My song is the song of the river
Calling for the open seas,
Wandering, wandering.

I am Life.

XVI

Love not the shapely branch,
Nor place its image alone in thy heart.
It dieth away.

Love the whole tree.
Then thou shalt love the shapely branch,
The tender and the withered leaf,
The shy bud and the full-blown flower,
The fallen petal and the dancing height,
The splendid shadow of full love.

Ah, love Life in its fullness.
It knoweth no decay.

XVII

Sorrow is soon forgotten
And pleasure is bound by tears.
None but the clear-eyed shall remember
The deep wounds of their passing sighs.

Sorrow is the shadow
In the wake of pleasure.
Desire is young in its anxious flight;
The swiftness of its deeds
Shall uncover the source of joy.

The conflict of discontent is suffering;
The inviting of sorrow
Is the way to happiness.

Life's dwelling place
Is in the heart of man.

XVIII

Ah, the symphony of that song!
The innermost shrine
Is breathless with the love of many.
The flame dances with the thoughts of many.

The scent of burnt camphor fills the air;
The careless priest drones a chant;
The idol sparkles, seeming to move,
Weary of such boundless adoration.

A still silence holds the air.
And on the instant
A melodious song of infinite heart
Brings untold tears to my eyes.

In a white robe
A woman sings to the heart of her love
Of the travail she knew not,
Of the laughter of children around her breast,
Of the love that died young,
Of the sorrow in a barren home,

Of the solitude in a still night,
Of life fruitless amidst the flowering earth.

I cry with her.
Her heart became mine.

She leaves that abode of sanctity,
Eager with the joy of worship on the morrow.

I follow her through the eternity of time.

O love,
Thou and I shall wander
On the open road of true love.
Thou and I shall never part.

XIX

I have lived the good and evil of men,
And dark became the horizon of my love.

I have known the morality and immorality of men,
And cruel became my anxious thought.

I have shared in the piety and impiety of men,
And heavy became the burden of life.

I have pursued the race of the ambitious,
And vain became the glory of life.

And now I have fathomed the secret purpose of desire.

XX

Out of the fullness of thy heart
Invite sorrow,
And the joy thereof shall be in abundance.

As the streams swell
After the great rains,
And the pebbles rejoice once again
In the murmur of running waters,
So shall thy wanderings by the wayside
Fill the emptiness that createth fear.
Sorrow shall unfold the weaving of Life;
Sorrow shall give the strength of loneliness;
Sorrow shall open unto thee
The closed doors of thy heart.

The cry of sorrow is the voice of fulfilment,
And the rejoicing therein
Is the fullness of Life.

XXI

I look to none beside Thee,
O my Beloved.
Thou art born in me,
And lo, there
I take my refuge.

I have read of Thee in many books.
They tell me
That there are many like unto Thee,
That many temples are built for Thee,
That there are many rites
To invoke Thee.
But I have no close communion with them.
For all these are but the shells
Of man's thoughts.

O friend,
Seek for the Well-beloved
In the secret recesses of thy heart.
Dead is the tabernacle
When the heart ceases to dance.

I look to none beside Thee,
O my Beloved.
Thou art born in me,
And lo, there
I take my refuge.

XXII

My brother died;
We were as two stars in a naked sky.

He was like me,
Burnt by the warm sun,
In the land where are soft breezes,
Swaying palms,
And cool rivers,
Where there are shadows numberless,
Bright-coloured parrots and chattering birds:

Where green tree-tops
Dance in the brilliant sun;
Where there are golden sands
And blue-green seas:

Where the world lives in the burden of the sun,
And the earth is baked dull brown;
Where the green-sparkling rice fields
Are luscious in slimy waters,
And shining, brown, naked bodies
Are free in the dazzling light:

The land
Of the mother suckling her babe by the road-
 side;
Of the devout lover
Offering gay flowers;
Of the wayside shrine;
Of intense silence;
Of immense peace.

He died;
I wept in loneliness.
Where'er I went, I heard his voice
And his happy laughter.
I looked for his face
In every passer-by,
And asked each if he had met with my
 brother;
But none could give me comfort.

I worshipped.
I prayed.
But the gods were silent.
I could weep no more;
I could dream no more.
I sought him in all things,
In every clime.

I heard the whispering of many trees,
Calling me to his abode.

And then,
In my search,
I beheld Thee,
O Lord of my heart;
In Thee alone
I saw the face of my brother.

In Thee alone,
O my eternal Love,
Do I behold the faces
Of all the living and all the dead.

XXIII

I tell thee
Orthodoxy is set up
When the mind and heart are in decay.

As the quiet pools of the wood
Lie hidden under a green mantle,
So is Life covered by the accumulation
Of autumnal thought.

As the soft leaf is heavy with the dust
Of last summer,
So is Life weary
With a dying love.

When thought and feeling are hedged about
By the fear of corruption,
Then, O friend,
Thou art caught up in the darkness
Of a fading day.

A tender leaf lies withering
In the shadow of a great valley.

XXIV

As a flower holds the scent,
So do I contain thee,
O World,
In my heart.

Keep me within thy heart;
For I am Liberation,
The unending happiness of Life.

As a precious stone
Lies deep in the earth,
So am I hidden
Deep in thy heart.

Though thou dost not know me
I know thee full well.
Though thou dost not think of me
My world is filled with thee.
Though thou dost not love me
Thou art my unchanging love.
Though thou worshippest me
In temples, churches and mosques,

I am a stranger to thee;
But thou art my eternal companion.
As the mountains protect
The peaceful valley,
So do I cover thee,
O World,
With the shadow of my hand.

As the rains come
To a parched land,
So, O World,
Do I come
With the scent of my love.

Keep thy heart
Pure and simple,
O World;
For then thou shalt welcome me.

I am thy love,
The desire of thy heart.

Keep thy mind
Tranquil and clear,
O World;
For therein is thine own understanding.

I am thine understanding,
The fullness
Of thine own experience.

I sit in the temple,
I sit by the wayside,
Watching the shadows move
From place to place.

XXV

Reason is the treasure of the mind,
Love is the perfume of the heart;
Yet both are of one substance,
Though cast in different moulds.

As a golden coin
Bears two images
Parted by a thin wall of metal,
So between love and reason
Is the poise of understanding,
That understanding
Which is of both mind and heart.

O Life, O Beloved,
In thee alone is eternal love,
In thee alone is everlasting thought.

XXVI

As the spark
That shall give warmth
Is hid among the grey ashes,
So, O friend,
The light
Which shall guide thee
Under the dust
Of thine experience.

XXVII

O friend,
Thou canst not bind Truth.

It is as the air,
Free, limitless,
Indestructible,
Immeasurable.

It hath no dwelling place,
Neither temple nor altar.
It is of no one God,
However zealous be His worshipper.

Canst thou tell
From what single flower
The bee gathereth the sweet honey?

O friend,
Leave heresy to the heretic,
Religion to the orthodox;
But gather Truth
From the dust of thine experience.

XXVIII

As the potter
To the joy of his heart
Moulds the clay;
So canst thou create
To the glory of thy being
Thy future.

As the man of the forest
Cuts a path
Through the thick jungle;
So canst thou make,
Through this turmoil of affliction,
A clear path
To thy freedom from sorrows,
To thy lasting happiness.

O friend,
As for a moment
The mysterious mountains
Are concealed by the passing mist;
So art thou hid

In the darkness
Of thy creation.
The fruit of the seed thou sowest
Shall burden thee.

O friend,
Heaven and hell
Are words
To frighten thee to right action;
But heaven and hell exist not.
Only the seeds of thine own actions
Shall bring into being
The flower of thy longing.

As the maker of images
Carves the human shape
Out of granite,
So, out of the rock
Of thine experience,
Hew thine eternal happiness.

Thy life is a death;
Death is a rebirth.
Happy is the man
That is beyond the clutches
Of their limitations.

XXIX

The mountain comes down to the dancing
 waters
But its head is hidden in a dark cloud.

On the stump of a dead pine
There grew a delicate flower.

The substance of my love is Life
And in its pathway there is no death.

XXX

Doubt is as a precious ointment;
Though it burns, it shall heal greatly.

I tell thee, invite doubt
When in the fullness of thy desire.
Call to doubt
At the time when thine ambition
Is outrunning others in thought.
Awaken doubt
When thy heart is rejoicing in great love.

I tell thee,
Doubt brings forth eternal love;
Doubt cleanses the mind of its corruption.
So the strength of thy days
Shall be established in understanding.

For the fullness of thy heart,
And for the flight of thy mind,
Let doubt tear away thine entanglements.

As the fresh winds from the mountains
That awaken the shadows in the valley,
So let doubt call to dance
The decaying love of a contented mind.

Let not doubt enter darkly thy heart.

I tell thee,
Doubt is as a precious ointment;
Though it burns, it shall heal greatly.

XXXI

Listen to me,
O friend.

Be thou a yogi, a monk, a priest,
A devout lover of God,
A pilgrim searching for happiness,
Bathing in holy rivers,
Visiting sacred shrines,
The occasional worshipper of a day,
A reader of many books,
Or a builder of temples,
My love aches for thee.
I know the way to the heart of the Beloved.

This vain struggle,
This long toil,
This ceaseless sorrow,
This changing pleasure,
This burning doubt,
This burden of life:
All these will cease, O friend.

My love aches for thee.
I know the way to the heart of the Beloved.

Have I wandered over the earth,
Have I loved the reflections,
Have I chanted, rapt in ecstasy,
Have I donned the robe,
Have I listened to the temple bells,
Have I grown heavy with study,
Have I searched,
Have I been lost?
Yea, much have I known.
My love aches for thee.
I know the way to the heart of the Beloved.

O friend,
Wouldst thou love the many reflections,
If thou canst have reality?
Throw away thy bells, thine incense,
Thy fears and thy gods;
Set aside thy creeds, thy philosophies;

Come,
Put aside all these:
I know the way to the heart of the Beloved.
O friend,
The simple union is the best.
That is the way to the heart of the Beloved.

XXXII

Through the veil of Form,
O Beloved,
I see Thee, myself in manifestation.

How unattainable are the mountains to the valley,
Though the mountains hold the valley!
How mysterious is the darkness
That brings forth the watching stars,
And yet the night is born of day!

I am in love with Life.
As the mountain lake
Which receives many streams
And sends forth great rivers,
But holds its unknown depths,
So is my love.

Calm and clear as the mountains in the morning
Is my thought,
Born of love.

Happy is the man who has found the harmony
 of Life,
For then he creates in the shadow of eternity.

Printed in the United States
42562LVS00004B